American Indians

The Navajo
A Proud People

Allison Lassieur

Enslow Elementary
an imprint of
Enslow Publishers, Inc.

40 Industrial Road   PO Box 38
Box 398   Aldershot
Berkeley Heights, NJ 07922   Hants GU12 6BP
USA   UK
http://www.enslow.com

794 3174

Editor's Note: We at Enslow Publishers, Inc., are aware that the people of the nation described in this book call themselves the Diné. However, since they are still often known as the Navajo, we have decided to use this term. We mean no disrespect to the Diné, but just wish to reach as many readers as possible in order to tell the rich history and current accomplishments of this vibrant people.

Enslow Elementary, an imprint of Enslow Publishers, Inc.

Enslow Elementary® is a registered trademark of Enslow Publishers, Inc.

Library of Congress Cataloging-in-Publication Data:

Lassieur, Allison.
    The Navajo : a proud people / Allison Lassieur.
      p. cm. — (American Indians)
    Includes bibliographical references and index.
    ISBN 0-7660-2453-9
    1. Navajo Indians—History—Juvenile literature. 2. Navajo Indians—Social life and customs—
Juvenile literature. I. Title. II. Series. III. American Indians (Berkeley Heights, N.J.)
    E99.N3L37 2005
    979.1004'9726—dc22

              2004016150

Printed in the United States of America

10 9 8 7 6 5 4 3 2 1

To Our Readers: We have done our best to make sure all Internet addresses in this book were active and appropriate when we went to press. However, the author and the publisher have no control over and assume no liability for the material available on those Internet sites or on other Web sites they may link to. Any comments or suggestions can be sent by e-mail to comments@enslow.com or to the address on the back cover.

Illustration Credits: Associated Press, ALBUQUERQUE JOURNAL, p. 26; Associated Press, AP, p. 40 Associated Press, THE DAILY HERALD, p. 32; Associated Press, THE GALLUP INDEPENDENT, pp. 5, 43; Clipart.com, pp. 14, 22, 28; Enslow Publishers, Inc., p. 6; © Corel Corporation, pp. 16, 29; Courtesy of the Mercaldo Archives, reproduced from *The Dictionary of American Portraits*, published by Dover Publications, Inc., in 1967, p. 38; Cpl. Paula M. Fitzgerald, Marine Corps, p. 37; David R. Frazier/The Image Works, p. 19; Gunnery Sgt. John Cordero, Marine Corps, p. 36; Jack Kurtz/The Image Works, pp. 8, 42; Jeff Greenberg/The Image Works, p. 20; Jim Noelker/The Image Works, p. 27; © Marilyn "Angel" Wynn/Nativestock.com, p. 1 (foreground), 12, 13, 15, 17, 18, 21, 23, 24, 25, 31, 33, 44; National Archives and Records Administration, pp. 1 (background), 9, 35; Photos.com, p. 7; Reproduced from the Collections of the Library of Congress, pp. 4, 39, 46; Topham/The Image Works, p. 30; Virginia Clark, R.C. Gorman Navajo Art Gallery, p. 41; Western History/Genealogy Dept., Denver Public Library, p. 34

Cover Illustration: © Marilyn "Angel" Wynn/Nativestock.com (foreground); National Archives and Records Administration (background).

Contents

The Code Talkers

In the early 1940s, World War II raged around the world. The Navajo played an important part in America's victory in this war.

In the late 1930s, Germany and Japan had invaded countries to get more land. Britain and France declared war on Germany. At first, the Americans stayed out of the war. But then Japan bombed an American naval base at Pearl Harbor, Hawaii, on December 7, 1941. The next day, the United States declared war.

By 1945, Germany had been defeated, but Japan was still fighting. In February, thousands of American forces attacked a Japanese island called Iwo Jima. Among the

Two Navajo Code Talkers send a message during World War II.

troops were six Navajo Marines. Their job: to transmit coded messages to other American forces in battle.

Huddled against bombs and gunfire, these six soldiers used their own Navajo language to send and receive more than eight hundred secret messages. The enemy was never able to figure out any of the messages. Later, their commander said that the Americans could never have defeated the Japanese at the Battle of Iwo Jima without the Navajo Code Talkers.

Navajo Code Talkers (back row) were present at the signing of a bill that called for a monument in their honor in the state of Arizona.

chapter one

The Land

The Navajo of the American Southwest call themselves Diné. *It means "the people." They call their homeland* Dinétah, *which means "among the people."*

The Navajo Then

Early Navajo people lived in the southwestern United States. The people were scattered in small villages or in nomadic bands. The Navajo became farmers and raised sheep. They grew crops such as corn. In the 1800s, the United States made

Navajo Lands

KEY:
◼ = Original Navajo Lands
☐ = Navajo Reservation
▲ = Mountain

COLORADO

Hesperus Peak

UTAH

▲ Blanca Peak

▲ Mount Taylor

San Francisco Peak ▲

ARIZONA

NEW MEXICO

N

According to Navajo history, their lands were between four peaks. Today, the land of the Navajo reservation covers much of their original land.

The land of the Navajo has interesting red rock formations.

the Navajo leave their homes. Later, the government allowed them to return. They have lived on the same lands ever since.

The Navajo Today

The Navajo lands, today called a reservation, cover about twenty-five thousand square miles of Arizona, Utah, and New Mexico. The capital of the Navajo Nation is Window Rock, Arizona.

Navajo lands include canyons, forests, and deserts. The forests are home to many types of trees such as Douglas fir, scrub oak, and aspen. Some desert plants such as Indian paintbrush and larkspur grow briefly in the spring. Small rodents, rabbits, snakes, insects, coyote, and deer live throughout Navajo lands.

chapter two

History

The Navajo people were almost all killed during the 1800s. Now they are one of the strongest American Indian groups.

Hundreds of years ago, the Navajo were hunters and gatherers. They traveled from place to place in search of food. Spanish explorers arrived in Navajo lands in the 1500s. They left horses and sheep behind. The Navajo learned to raise sheep and ride horses. They also learned how to grow crops. The

The Navajo have always raised farm animals. This modern Navajo herds goats in Arizona.

This group photo was taken of some of the survivors of the "Long Walk" in 1864.

Navajo stopped traveling the land in search of food. Instead, they moved between summer and winter camps and began raising their own food.

In the 1800s, Mexicans started taking Navajo women and children as slaves. The Navajo fought back. In 1864, the United States decided to force the Navajo onto a reservation in New Mexico to stop the bloodshed. A military scout named Kit Carson and his men began burning Navajo homes, destroying crops, and killing livestock. Thousands of starving Navajo surrendered and were forced to take part in what came to be known as the "Long Walk."

About eight thousand Navajo were forced to walk three hundred miles to Fort Sumner in eastern New Mexico. This became known as the "Long Walk." More than three hundred Navajo died on the Long Walk. Four years later, the United States government admitted that they had made a mistake. They signed a treaty with the Navajo in 1868. This treaty allowed the Navajo to return to many of their original lands. Their lands were now overseen by the American government and were called a reservation.

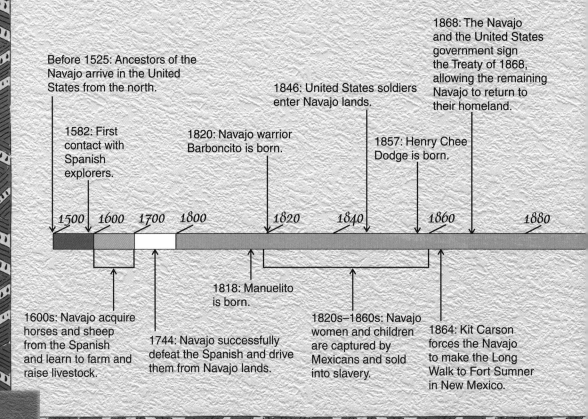

Before 1525: Ancestors of the Navajo arrive in the United States from the north.

1582: First contact with Spanish explorers.

1820: Navajo warrior Barboncito is born.

1846: United States soldiers enter Navajo lands.

1857: Henry Chee Dodge is born.

1868: The Navajo and the United States government sign the Treaty of 1868, allowing the remaining Navajo to return to their homeland.

1500   1600   1700   1800   1820   1840   1860   1880

1818: Manuelito is born.

1600s: Navajo acquire horses and sheep from the Spanish and learn to farm and raise livestock.

1744: Navajo successfully defeat the Spanish and drive them from Navajo lands.

1820s–1860s: Navajo women and children are captured by Mexicans and sold into slavery.

1864: Kit Carson forces the Navajo to make the Long Walk to Fort Sumner in New Mexico.

It took many years for the Navajo to recover from their losses. Slowly they grew. In the 1920s, coal and oil were discovered on the Navajo reservation. This brought much-needed money to the Navajo. Over the years, they have added land to their reservation. Today, most Navajo still live and work on the reservation. Many families continue to farm and to raise sheep and goats. Some Navajo make beautiful crafts. Other Navajo live and work in large cities around the United States.

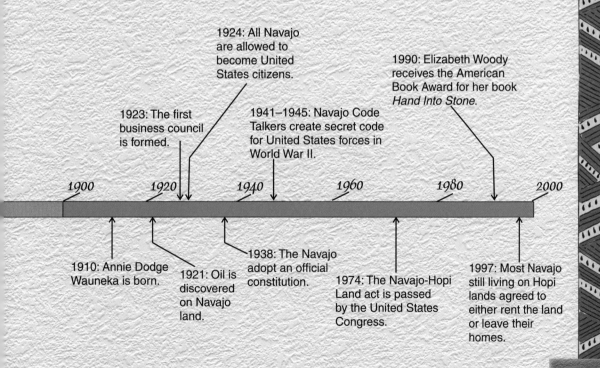

1924: All Navajo are allowed to become United States citizens.

1990: Elizabeth Woody receives the American Book Award for her book *Hand Into Stone*.

1923: The first business council is formed.

1941–1945: Navajo Code Talkers create secret code for United States forces in World War II.

1900   1920   1940   1960   1980   2000

1910: Annie Dodge Wauneka is born.

1921: Oil is discovered on Navajo land.

1938: The Navajo adopt an official constitution.

1974: The Navajo-Hopi Land act is passed by the United States Congress.

1997: Most Navajo still living on Hopi lands agreed to either rent the land or leave their homes.

chapter three

Homes

The home is very important to the Navajo. They have a special blessing called a "Navajo house blessing" that is done for every new home.

The Navajo Then

Years ago, Navajo families lived in traditional round homes called hooghans. Hooghan is a Navajo word that means "the place home." (These homes are sometimes called "hogans," too.) The frame for

The traditional hoogan had earth piled on top of its roof.

the hooghan was built out of logs. The wood was covered with packed mud and earth. Sometimes the hooghans were shaped like cones. Other hooghans might have had six or eight sides. All hooghans were built with their doorways facing east, toward the rising sun. Some families had an open work space with a flat roof and no walls. Many families would store food and belongings in other small buildings.

The Navajo Today

Most Navajo live in modern houses today. However, they still build hooghans the same way their ancestors did long ago. Many sacred Navajo ceremonies can only be done

In the center of this hooghan is a fire pit. The fire's smoke goes out the hole in the ceiling. In the background, are looms for weaving.

inside a hooghan. It is not unusual to see a modern house and a hooghan side by side on the Navajo reservation.

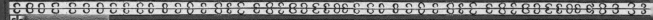

chapter four

Clothing

Clothing and cloth have been important to the Navajo for hundreds of years. They are known for their colorful clothing and rich jewelry.

The Navajo Then

Early Navajo wore leggings, skirts, and blankets woven from cedar bark and yucca plants. They also wore clothing and shoes made of animal skins. In the 1800s, white settlers and explorers brought cloth such as wool and cotton for trade. Navajo men and women began wearing clothing made of cloth. Men's buckskin pants were often

In this painting by Louise Berkencamp, a Navajo woman wears a woven blanket.

decorated with brass and silver buttons. They had woolen leggings dyed bright blue. Women wore leggings made of strips of buckskin decorated with silver buttons.

The Navajo Today

Today, most Navajo wear clothing like jeans, T-shirts, dresses, and suits. However, they still wear traditional clothing for special ceremonies and cultural events. Traditional Navajo clothing is very much like the clothing from the past. Women tie brightly-colored sashes around their waists. Both men and women wear beautiful jewelry made of silver, turquoise, and shells.

A Navajo father and daughter sing and play music. She is wearing a wool dress and silver and turquoise jewelry. Her hair is tied with feathers. He wears a headdress.

chapter five

Food and Meals

The Navajo people have always known how to live off the land and make the most of the food they find.

The Navajo Then

Hundreds of years ago, the Navajo hunted deer and prairie dog for food. They also picked and ate wild fruits and vegetables. In the 1600s, other American Indian tribes taught the Navajo how to grow crops such as corn, beans, and squash. The Navajo began raising sheep and goats that had been left behind by Spanish explorers.

By the 1800s, the Navajo ate dishes such as mush made from corn, seeds,

After the Navajo learned how to grow corn and squash, they became the main part of their daily diet.

and goat's milk. Another common dish was fry bread. Fry bread is a plate-sized circle of wheat bread fried in hot fat. The Navajo also ate mutton (sheep).

The Navajo Today

A modern Navajo family eats much the same foods that other Americans enjoy. Most Navajo no longer farm for a living. They work other jobs so they will have enough money to live. Some Navajo continue to farm the land. Most of them raise cattle instead of sheep. People still prepare traditional foods for ceremonies and special occasions.

This Navajo woman demonstrates how to grind dried corn with a stone. Corn that is ground into a powder is called corn meal. It can then be used to make bread or tortillas.

chapter six

Family Life

The Navajo have always found strength in their families.

The Navajo Then

In the 1800s, the Navajo lived in small groups of several families. Each group was known as a clan. These clans worked together to grow crops and to gather food. Not all

Sisters Erin (left) and Amber Foster make fancy bead designs.

Three generations of Navajo family

members of a clan were related to one another. However, everyone in a clan was considered to be part of a large, extended family. All Navajo children belonged to their mother's clan. The Navajo could not marry anyone from their own clan. Instead, they looked to other clans to find a husband or wife. Most Navajo marriages were arranged by the families and the clans.

A father teaches his son how to make jewelry at the New Mexico State fair.

The Navajo Today

The Navajo people are still divided into clans. Today there are more than eighty Navajo clans. Each clan owns farm fields and sheep herds. The groups are further divided into households. Each married couple has its own household within the clan.

When a Navajo man and woman marry, they can choose to live with the woman's group or the man's group. They are welcomed by either family. In recent years, many Navajo couples have chosen to live on their own, near their jobs.

Children are very important to the Navajo. Older

Navajo teach children by telling them stories. The stories teach Navajo children about their history. The stories also teach children important lessons. Older children learn how to do different jobs. Boys learn how to herd and hunt. Girls learn how to cook and weave. Navajo children also play the same sports and games as most other American children.

These two brothers and their sister are all in the same Navajo clan.

chapter seven

Everyday Life

Yesterday or today, the daily life of the Navajo has always been exciting.

The Navajo Then

Long ago, a Navajo's day revolved around growing food and herding sheep. In the morning, Navajo men left to care for the sheep. They taught their sons how to do this as well. Other Navajo men might spend the day hunting for game such as deer and prairie dog.

The women gathered and prepared the food for the day. Later, a woman might work on a rug she was weaving, while another might finish a basket or pot

In addition to herding sheep, the Navajo cut off the sheeps' wool in a process called shearing. They then use the wool to make thread for weaving.

While Navajo women worked, they often carried their babies in cradleboards. Today, some mothers still use cradleboards.

she had been making. Navajo girls learned from their mothers how to do these tasks as well.

The Navajo Today

The lives of modern Navajo are a mix of modern and traditional. Most children go to school. In addition to subjects taught in American schools, they are also taught the Navajo language and history. Some Navajo adults leave for jobs in nearby towns, while others continue to farm their land and herd sheep. Many women have jobs outside the home, while others make a living by making blankets and pottery.

chapter eight

Religion and Medicine

In the Navajo culture, religion and medicine are very closely linked together.

The Navajo Then

Long ago, the Navajo believed that they should keep harmony and balance with nature and with other people.

Four Navajo perform the gourd dance in Phoenix, Arizona.

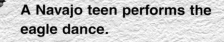

A Navajo teen performs the eagle dance.

The Navajo have a word for this idea: hózho. Hózho means this idea of harmony, goodness, and beauty with the world.

The Navajo performed many special ceremonies to make sure that the world stayed in hózho. These ceremonies were used to bring harmony back into the world if something had gone wrong. The ceremonies might include sand painting, singing, or dancing. Some ceremonies included the use of sacred objects wrapped in a bundle.

The Navajo Today

Many modern Navajo follow religions such as Christianity. However, they also continue to believe in their traditional religion. For instance, the ancient belief of hózho has carried into the present day. It is not

Shawn Price, a Navajo, became a member of the Jewish religion. He is playing an instrument called the shofar.

uncommon for a Navajo to follow the teachings of more than one religion. Modern Navajo religion also includes events called Blessingway rites. These are used for many occasions to give hope, good luck, and blessings for a long, happy life. Navajo ceremonies are usually conducted by a special person called hataali, or a singer. Singing is a very important part of each ritual. Navajo hataali are respected members of the tribe. They train for many years. Most hataali are men, although a few women have also become Navajo hataali as well.

Margaret Edgewater is a Navajo medicine woman. She searches for herbs to help heal the sick.

Navajo ceremonies are often used for curing sickness and disease. Herbs are still gathered and used to heal the sick. Today, some modern hospitals, especially in the areas where many Navajo live, allow hataali to perform ceremonies for patients who want them.

chapter nine

Arts and Music

Over hundreds of years, the Navajo have developed their own unique arts and music.

The Navajo Then

Art has been a part of Navajo life for hundreds of years. Many of their legends and stories include descriptions of weaving and other arts. It is thought that the Navajo most likely learned to weave from neighboring Pueblo tribes sometime in the late 1600s.

In the past, weaving was one of the more important arts of the

Two Navajo women work together to weave a rug.

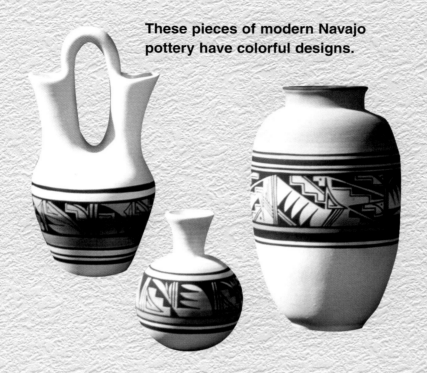

These pieces of modern Navajo pottery have colorful designs.

Navajo people. During the 1800s, Navajo women wove beautiful blankets with designs such as stripes and diamonds. One blanket or rug might take hundreds of hours to make.

Basketry is another Navajo art. Many Navajo ceremonies use special baskets to hold sacred objects or foods. Baskets are often decorated with star designs, curved patterns, or figures of humans and animals. A well-known type of Navajo basket is called a "wedding

A Navajo medicine man works on a sacred piece of art called a sand painting.

basket." These are shallow, plate-like baskets woven with beautiful designs in many different colors.

Music is a very important part of Navajo life. The hataali often perform many special songs during Navajo ceremonies. These people also sing Navajo lullabies, children's songs, and funny songs. Many times Navajo songs are accompanied by rattles, drums, and other musical instruments.

The Navajo Today

Navajo women continue to make beautiful blankets and rugs that sell for thousands of dollars. For many Navajo families, weaving is their main source of income.

Many modern Navajo are experts at working with

This bracelet is made of turquoise and silver.

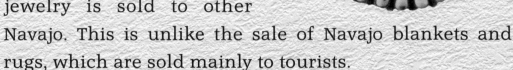

silver. Artists craft beautiful jewelry out of silver and turquoise. Much of this jewelry is sold to other Navajo. This is unlike the sale of Navajo blankets and rugs, which are sold mainly to tourists.

Today the Navajo listen to all kinds of music, including pop, rock, and country. Navajo children also like hip-hop, metal, and reggae.

This modern Navajo blanket shows a western scene.

chapter ten

Sports and Games

The Navajo have discovered new sports and games to play, while keeping the old traditions alive.

The Navajo Then

In the past, the Navajo played traditional games such as the moccasin, or shoe, game. The moccasin game was based on a Navajo story. In the story, night creatures and day creatures fought over who had the most power. Each group wanted it to be either day or night all the time. So they played a game.

In the game, a ball made of stone was hidden in one of four moccasins. Each team

Modern Navajo like to play basketball.

had to guess which shoe the ball was hidden in. Loaves of yucca bread were used to keep score. The team who guessed correctly the most times won.

The Navajo have excelled in riding horses. Today, they compete in rodeos.

The Navajo Today

Many Navajo children still play the moccasin game. However, they also enjoy other games and sports such as basketball, football, and baseball. Navajo girls and boys participate in track and swimming.

Girls' volleyball is a popular sport. Rodeos are very popular in the Navajo community. Navajo children also love computer games.

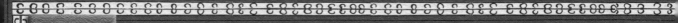

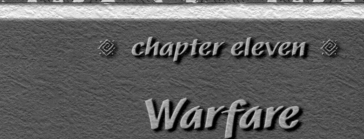

chapter eleven
Warfare

The Navajo have defended themselves when they needed to. They have also joined the military to help defend the United States of America.

The Navajo Then

Hundreds of years ago, the Navajo battled the Spanish explorers who entered their lands. In the 1800s, they fought neighboring tribes for land and sheep. In the 1820s, the Navajo became targets for attack by the Mexicans who lived in New Mexico. These

In this photo from the late 1800s, a warrior holds his bow and arrows.

Mexicans captured Navajo women and children and sold them as slaves. The Navajo fought back against the Mexicans for many years.

In the 1850s, American soldiers came to Navajo lands. They tried to sign treaties with the Navajo. But the Navajo and the soldiers did not always understand each other. The soldiers did not help the Navajo when the Mexicans made their people slaves. Soldiers and Navajo fought one another. Finally, the soldiers rounded up the Navajo and forced them onto a reservation.

The Navajo Today

During the twentieth century, Navajo soldiers fought in many American wars, including World War I, World War II, Vietnam, and recent conflicts. The Navajo Code Talkers of World War II are the most famous Navajo soldiers.

Three Code Talkers take a break on the island of Saipan.

Nelson Draper, Sr., and Joe Morris were Navajo Code Talkers. They are waiting to receive the Silver Medal Award for their service in World War II.

During World War II, United States forces needed a secret code that the Japanese could not understand. A soldier named Philip Johnston had the idea to use the Navajo language as a secret code. He convinced military officers to try it. Twenty-nine Navajo men joined the marines and created a special code using words from their own language. During battle, the Code Talkers' job was to send secret messages between fighting troops. The Japanese never broke the code. Because of this, the Code Talkers kept thousands of U.S. soldiers safe during the war. Today, the few living veteran Code Talkers are some of the Navajo's most respected elders. They have also been honored with Silver Medal Awards by the government of the United States.

Corporal Kayelee Yazzie is a Navajo woman in the Marines. Her father served in the Vietnam War and her grandfather served in World War II. She is serving in Iraq.

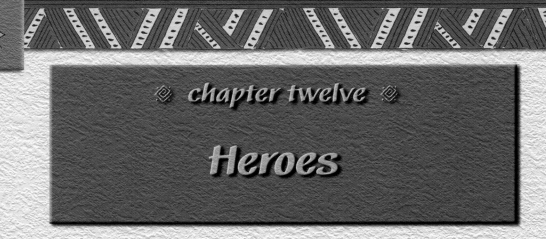

chapter twelve

Heroes

Navajo heroes include strong leaders, as well as great artists, writers, and activists.

The Navajo Then

The Navajo have many famous and notable people in their history. Manuelito was born in 1818. He and his warriors were the last Navajo to surrender to Kit Carson. After the Long Walk, Manuelito continued to serve as a leader of the Navajo. He led them back to their homelands when they were released.

Henry Chee Dodge was born in about 1857. He was only

Manuelito was among the last to surrender to Kit Carson (pictured).

Manuelito had his portrait taken in the 1870s.

about eight years old when he went on the Long Walk. Later, he grew to become a strong leader. When Manuelito died, Henry Chee Dodge was chosen to be the Navajo's head chief. He worked hard to create a strong government for his people.

Annie Dodge Wauneka was the daughter of Henry Chee Dodge. She was born in 1910. Annie Wauneka was the first woman to be elected to the Navajo Tribal Council.

Dr. Annie Wauneka (second from right) was honored as a *Ladies Home Journal* Woman of the Year in 1976.

She began a health education program for the tribe. In December 1963, Annie Wauneka was the first American Indian to be awarded the Presidential Medal of Freedom.

The Navajo Today

Some modern Navajo heroes include Elizabeth Woody and R. C. Gorman. Elizabeth Woody is a well-known

Navajo poet. She has published several award-winning books, including *Hand into Stone* and *Seven Hands, Seven Hearts.* R. C. Gorman is one of the most famous Navajo sculptors. He was the first living American Indian artist to have his works shown in the Metropolitan Museum of Art in New York. Today he has a successful art gallery in Taos, New Mexico.

R. C. Gorman has a gallery in Taos, New Mexico.

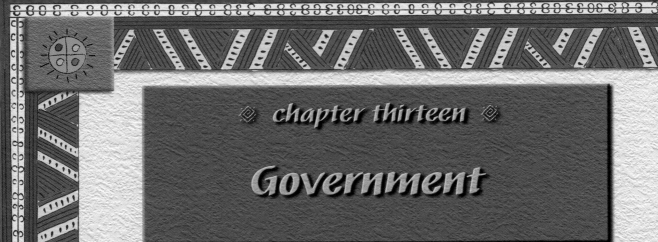

chapter thirteen

Government

The Navajo believe that every person has a right to speak for himself or herself. They also believe that the group has no right to force a person to do something.

The Navajo Then

In the past, there was no head chief of the entire tribe. Most Navajo lived in small groups with a headman as leader. Sometimes several groups might come together under one local headman. This headman was in charge of warfare and negotiation with other groups. These leaders signed peace treaties to end wars.

Peter MacDonald was once chairman of the Navajo Nation. Here, he and his wife and daughter ride in a parade on their reservation.

The Navajo Nation Council listens to Arizona governor Janet Napolitano (lower left, center) speak in 2003.

In 1921, the United States government wanted to drill for oil on Navajo lands, but there was no overall Navajo leader to ask for permission. So, the Navajo created a business council in 1923. They worked with the American government to give the United States mining and oil rights on Navajo lands. Many historians and Navajo think that the deal was unfair to the Navajo.

The Navajo Today

The Navajo decided to continue to use councils. The Navajo also have a tribal president and courts of law, including a Supreme Court. Elections are held every four years in November.

Old and New

The Navajo tribe was almost destroyed in the 1800s. Today, the Navajo are among the most successful American Indian tribes in the United States. They have worked hard for this success. Modern Navajo culture is a mix of old beliefs and new ideas. The Navajo people continue to respect their history. They teach their children the Navajo language. Schools teach traditional culture. Traditional spiritual beliefs and ceremonies are part of the daily lives of many Navajo.

But the people are also good at accepting new ideas. They have found ways to combine their history and beliefs with the modern world. They have adapted to many changes without losing the Navajo way of life. This is one of their greatest strengths.

A Navajo boy feeds his pet sheep.

Words to Know

adapt—To make fit for a specific use.

ancestor—A person from whom one is descended.

ceremony—An act performed according to certain customs.

Diné—Navajo word that means "the people."

Dinétah—The Navajo name for their homeland, it means "among the people."

government—A group of people who make laws.

hataali—Medicine men; ceremonial singers of the Navajo.

hooghan—A Navajo home that is often round and made of logs and mud. Its doorway faces east towards the sunrise. The word means "the place home" in the Navajo language.

hózho—A Navajo word that describes the idea of harmony, goodness, and beauty with the world.

reservation—Land reserved for an American Indian group's own use.

traditional—Relating to a tradition.

More Books!

Bial, Raymond. *The Long Walk: The Story of Navajo Captivity.* New York: Benchmark Books, 2003.

Bishop, Amanda and Bobbie Kalman. *Life of the Navajo.* New York: Crabtree Publication Company, 2004.

DeAngelis, Therese. *The Navajo: Weavers of the Southwest.* Mankato: Minn.: Blue Earth Books, 2004.

McIntosh, Kenneth. *Navajo.* Philadelphia: Mason Crest Publishers, 2004.

Rosinsky, Natalie M. *The Navajo.* Minneapolis. Compass Point Books, 2005.

Santella, Andrew. *Navajo Code Talkers.* Minneapolis: Compass Point Books, 2004.

Internet Addresses

The American West: The Navajo

<http://www.americanwest.com>

Click on "Indians" at the left. Click on "Native American Nations' Homepages," then "Navajo Nation's Main Home Page."

Navajo Art

<http://www.un.org>

Click on "CyberSchoolBus" link. Click on "Indigenous People" at the right under the "Curriculum" heading. At the left, click on "Appreciate Navajo Art."

Navajo Code Talkers

<http://www.history.navy.mil>

Click on the "Frequently Asked Questions" button. Scroll down and select "Code Talkers, World War II."

Index

RAP

GAYLORD FG